RHYMED RUMINATIONS

RHYMED RUMINATIONS

by

SIEGFRIED SASSOON

FABER AND FABER LIMITED
24 Russell Square
London

FIRST PUBLISHED IN OCTOBER MCMXL
BY FABER AND FABER LIMITED
24 RUSSELL SQUARE LONDON W.C.I.
PRINTED IN GREAT BRITAIN BY
THE CHISWICK PRESS LTD LONDON

To

EDMUND BLUNDEN

CONTENTS

7

BREVITIES

I am that man who with a luminous look
Sits up at night to write a ruminant book.

I am that man who with a furrowing frown
Thinks harshly of the world—and corks it down.

I am that man who loves to ride alone
When landscapes wear his mind's autumnal tone.

I am that man who, having lived his day,
Looks once on life and goes his wordless way.

THOUGHTS IN 1932

Alive—and forty-five—I jogged my way
Across a dull green day,
Listening to larks and plovers, well content
With the pre-Roman pack-road where I went.

Pastoral and pleasant was the end of May.
But readers of the times had cause to say
That skies were brighter for the late Victorians;
And 'The Black Thirties' seemed a sobriquet
Likely to head the chapters of historians.

Above Stonehenge a drone of engines drew
My gaze; there seven and twenty war-planes flew
Manoeuvring in formation; and the drone
Of that neat-patterned hornet-gang was thrown
Across the golden downland like a blight.

Cities, I thought, will wait them in the night
When airmen, with high-minded motives, fight
To save Futurity. In years to come
Poor panic-stricken hordes will hear that hum,
And Fear will be synonymous with Flight.

PROPERTY

Upstairs among my books
I heard a noise of rooks
Returning to the woods.
Loud was that legion wheeling;
And queer my inward feeling—
'These windows are revealing
My chattels and my goods.'

Possession thus we claim
Of natural sights and sounds,
Who purchase earth with pounds
And take it all for granted.
We nothings use a name,
Nor ask whence acorns came
Before the oak was planted.

OUTLIVED BY TREES

A beech, a cedar, and a lime
Grow on my lawn, embodying time.
A lime, a cedar, and a beech
The transience of this lifetime teach.
    Beech, cedar, lime, when I'm dead Me,
    You'll stand, lawn-shadowing, tree by tree;
    And in your greenery, while you last,
    I shall survive who shared your past.

EULOGY OF MY HOUSE

House, though you've harboured grave-yards-full of lives
Since on your first foundations walls were built,
In your essential atmosphere survives
No sense of men's malignity and guilt.
Bad times you must have known, and human wrongness;
Yet your plain wisdom leaves it all behind you,
Within whose walls tranquillity and strongness
Keep watch on life. Dependable I find you.

Much good has been your making. I can feel
That when your ghosts revisit you they steal
From room to room like moonlight long ago:
And if some voice from silence haunts my head
I only wonder who it was that said—
'House, I am here because I loved you so.'

IN HEYTESBURY WOOD

Not less nor more than five and forty years ago
The old lord went along the ornamental ride;
For the last time he walked there, tired and very slow;
Saw the laburnum's golden chains, the glooming green
Of bowery box-trees; stood and looked farewell, and sighed
For roots that held his heart and summers that he'd seen.

And then, maybe, he came again there, year by year,
To watch, as dead men do, and see—who knows how clear?—
That vista'd paradise which in his time had thriven;
Those trees to which in cogitating strolls he'd given
Perennial forethought,—branches that he'd lopped and
    cherished:
Came, and saw sad neglect; dense nettles; favourites felled
Or fallen in gales and left to rot; came and beheld
How with succeeding seasons his laburnums perished.

'Return', I think, 'next summer, and you'll find such
    change,—
Walking, some low-lit evening, in the whispering wood,—
As will refresh your eyes and do them ghostly good;
See redolence befriend, neglect no more estrange;
See plumed acacia and the nobly tranquil bay;
Laburnums too, now small as in the prosperous prime
Of your well-ordered distant mid-Victorian time . . .'
    Thus I evoke him; thus he looks and goes his way
    Along that path we call the ornamental ride—
    The old slow lord, the ghost whose trees were once his
        pride.

WHILE READING A GHOST STORY

Opening my window for a breath of air
I meet the midnight cold, and am aware
Of wind-shook trees and harmless lonely stars.
There's nothing monstrous moving; nothing mars
This friendly blustering of mid-winter gloom.
   Behind me, in the comfort of my room,
   A story I've been reading lies half read . . .
   Corrupt revisitation by the dead.

Old houses have their secrets. Passions haunt them.
When day's celestials go, abhorred ones taunt them.
Inside our habitations darkness dwells.
While dusk of dawn is on the unwatched stair
And lofty windows whiten strangely,—there
What presence thins—with what frustrated spells?

ON EDINGTON HILL

Stars wink beyond the downland barrows
Where Alfred marched to meet the Danes,
Far in advance of flinthead arrows
And unaware of aeroplanes.

Now the white owl on silent wing
Crosses the looming lonely track;
And here our anti-pagan king
Beat the red-handed plunderers back.

That Eastertide—historians write—
He saved the future by the sword
Which emblemed in barbaric night
The cross of Jesus Christ his Lord.
That was the crucial point, men say:
For Alfred's wisdom was his crown,
Who, in the old skull-shattering way,
Christened the powers of darkness down.

Dawn breaks where tribes once fought with flints;
Where Alfred smote, the white owl flits
Whose instincts are as old as time.
And we—to-day's historian hints—
May all be Alfreds, bombed to bits
In conflict with a creed of crime.

1935.

878-1935

Here, on his march to Eathundun, King Alfred passed:
No wood was planted then; the terraced hill was grassed.
Now, in the summer, tanks come lumbering down the lane.
I'd like to watch King Alfred walk this way again.

Then, it was quite correct to hack and hew the Dane,
And to be levied for a war was life's event.
Now in a world of books I try to live content,
And hear uneasily the droning aeroplane.

I'd rather die than be some dim ninth-century thane;
Nor do I envy those who fought at Eathundun.
Yet I have wondered, when was Wiltshire more insane
Than now—when world ideas like wolves are on the run?

SILVER JUBILEE CELEBRATION

(At the Dinner of the Royal Society of St. George)

Broadcast across the as yet unbeaconed dark,
I heard the shout of that symposiarch
Whose voice, like some Gargantuan-mouthed grotesque,
Demanded silence for the honoured guest.
Then—when prolonged applauding had subsided—
Kipling, that legendary name, confided
In us—a host of atmospheric ears—
His planned post-mortem on the post-war years.

Suavely severe—not one bleak syllable blurred—
In dulcet-bitter and prophetic tones
(Each word full charged with dynamite deferred)
He disinterred a battlefield of bones. . . .
And then reminded us that our attempt
To put all war behind us with the last one
Had been a dream administrators dreamt;
In fact a virtuous fallacy—and a vast one.

Meanwhile his audience, mystified at first,
Sat spell-bound while he preached with barbed conviction,
Who, through implied anathemas, re-cursed
Our old opponents in that four years friction.
And if indeed it was the astringent truth
He told with such incomparable concision—
That we must now re-educate our youth
With 'Arm or perish' as their ultimate vision—

Let us at least be candid with the world
And stitch across each Union Jack unfurled
'No bargain struck with Potsdam is put over
Unless well backed by bombers—and Jehovah!'

A REMEMBERED QUEEN

If I could see that wild and warring Queen
Who lived here for a time, old histories claim;
If she, revisioned by my thought, could come!

Did voices walk the air, released from death,
Hers might be heard when, very late at night,
I turn the wireless on and catch no sound
But atmospheric cracklings, moans, and thuds.
Hers might be heard, associate with this ground
Whereon her house once stood. Eight hundred years
Are not so far, in terms of light from star.

Like moonlight on the low mist in the park
Is that remembered fierce twelfth-century Queen
Who lived here once, men say. If on the dark
I heard shrill Norman French and stood between
That utterance and eternity! If, so
Attuned, I could watch Queen Matilda go
Hunched on her horse across the crunching snow!

PREHISTORIC BURIALS

These barrows of the century-darkened dead,—
Memorials of oblivion, these turfed tombs
Of muttering ancestries whose fires, once red,
Now burn for me beyond mysterious glooms;
   I pass them day by day while daylight fills
   My sense of sight on these time-haunted hills.

Could I but watch those burials that began
Whole history—flint and bronze and iron beginnings,
When under this wide Wiltshire sky crude man
Warred with his world and augured our world-winnings!
Could I but enter that unholpen brain,
Cabined and comfortless and insecure,
That ruled some settlement on Salisbury Plain
And offered blood to blind primeval powers,—
Dim Caliban whose doom was to endure
Earth's ignorant nullity made strange with flowers.

ANTIQUITIES

Enormous aqueducts have had their day,
And moles make mounds where marshals camped and
   clashed.
On stones where awe-struck emperors knelt to pray
The tourist gapes with guide-book, unabashed.
Historian Time, who in his 'Life of Man'
Records the whole, himself is much unread:
The breath must go from beauty, and the span
Of Lethe bleaken over all the dead.

Only the shattered arch remains to tell
Humanity its transience and to be
Life-work for archaeologists who spell
The carven hieroglyphics of Chaldee.
And where the toiling town once seethed in smoke
There'll drop, through quiet, one acorn from an oak.

A LOCAL TRAIN OF THOUGHT

Alone, in silence, at a certain time of night,
Listening, and looking up from what I'm trying to write,
I hear a local train along the Valley. And 'There
Goes the one-fifty', think I to myself; aware
That somehow it's habitual travelling comforts me,
Making my world seem safer, homelier, sure to be
The same to-morrow; and the same, one hopes, next year.
'There's peacetime in that train.' One hears it disappear
With needless warning whistle and rail-resounding wheels.
'That train's quite like an old familiar friend', one feels.

THOUGHTS IN 1938

A man's mood can be not unlike the place, the time of day,
  the weather:
One afternoon, toward sundown, these were toned for me,
  all three together.
Riding with ruminant mind, I stared at Salisbury Plain's
  November distance,
By solitude imbued, responsive to my world without
  resistance.

Mild weather after wind and rain; earth, sky, and season all
  quiescent.
'If this be my biography,' I mused, 'to pace along is pleasant;
And after all, my unambitious mid-maturity deserves
—If luck befriends me thus—this liberal landscape's con-
  tour lines and curves.'

There on that ancient drove-road, leading to nowhere now,
  my horse
Grazed and then gazed, as I did, over the quietly coloured
  miles.
Though sign-posts pointed toward the dread of war, ourselves, of course,
Were only humdrum joggers on through time. Remembering it one smiles.

'A VIEW OF OLD EXETER'

Pyne, a small honest painter, well content
To limn our English landscapes, worked and went,
From 1800 onward, seventy years,
Then left the world to louden in men's ears.
Here's his 'Old Exeter'; much eyed by me
Since (how time flits!) full fifteen years ago
I bought it cheap and carried it home to be
A window on my wall making me know
Old Exeter, affectionately recorded
In the now slow paced 'fifties.
                                    Glancing down
From some neglected meadow near the town,
He hummed and sketched that I might be afforded
This purview of the past's provincial peace.

For J. B. Pyne Old Exeter was good;
Cows in his foreground grazed and strolled and stood:
For J. B. Pyne Victorian clumps of trees
Were golden in a bland October breeze:
Large clouds, like safe investments, loitered by;
And distant Dartmoor loomed in sombre blue.
Perpetuator of that shifting sky,
It never crossed his mind that he might do
From death such things as make me stare and sigh,—
Sigh for that afternoon he thus depicted,—
That simpler world from which we've been evicted.

Here his prim figures cruise and sit and drive

In crinolines as when they were alive.
Out of the town that man and wife are going
In smart new gig, complacently unknowing
Of their great-grandchild's air-raid-worried mind:
Into the town those gentlewomen are walking
Attuned to life, of the new Bishop talking—
Pleased that the eighteenth century's left behind,
And civically unconscious, I conjecture,
Of what it gave them in good architecture.
That group beside the cypresses adds calm
And absent-minded momentary charm
To the industrious artist's composition . . .
    When J. B. Pyne's, this was a Devon Day.
    For me it shines far far—too far—away;
    For time has changed this 'View' into a Vision.

METAMORPHOSIS

Sandys sat translating Ovid. Both his hands
Were busy. Busy was his curious mind.
Each note he wrote was news from fabled lands.
He hob-nobbed with Pythagoras, calm and kind.
In a quaint narrow age, remote from this,
Sat Sandys translating *Metamorphosis*.

The scholarship is obsolete, and the verse
Pedestrian perhaps. Yet, while I turn
His friendly folio pages (none the worse
For emblematic worm-holes) I discern
Not Nature preying on itself, but Time
Revealed by rich humanity in rhyme.

IDEOLOGIES

'I've an idea!' cried someone long ago
In liveliest monkey-language. What he thought
Caused chatter. What it was we do not know.
But this was the earliest ape on earth who brought
Experimental notions into play.
Nature ignored him, as she does to-day.

When Man's at last learnt how to make his mind
Nature may listen to thought and serve its needs.
Meanwhile where Babels once were built we find
A spider in his web among the weeds.

TWO OLD LADIES

Here's an old lady, almost ninety-one.
Fragile in dark blue velvet, from her chair
She talks to me about Lord Palmerston,
With whom her father 'often took the air'.
I watch her tiny black-lace-mittened hands—
When tea-time's ended—slowly crumble a rusk
For feeding peacocks with. Reflective stands
My memory-mirror in the autumn dusk.

Memory records the scene; and straightway plays
One of its dream-like unexpected tricks;
Transports me forty years to summer days
On time's first page, when I was only six. . . .
Miss Clara, deaf and old, alert and queer,
With scraps of bread heaped on a dark blue dish,
Conducts me—I can catch her voice quite clear—
Out to the lily-pond to feed the fish.

BLUNDEN'S BEECH

I named it Blunden's Beech; and no one knew
That this—of local beeches—was the best.
Remembering lines by Clare, I'd sometimes rest
Contentful on the cushioned moss that grew
Between its roots. Finches, a flitting crew,
Chirped their concerns. Wiltshire, from east to west,
Contained my tree. And Edmund never guessed
How he was there with me till dusk and dew.

Thus, fancy-free from ownership and claim,
The mind can make its legends live and sing
And grow to be the genius of some place.
And thus, where sylvan shadows held a name,
The thought of Poetry will dwell, and bring
To summer's idyll an unheeded grace.

NOVEMBER DUSK

Ruminant, while firelight glows on shadowy walls
And dusk with the last leaves of autumn falls,
I hear my garden thrush whose notes again
Tell stillness after hours of gusty rain.

Can I record tranquillity intense
With harmony of heart,—experience
Like a rich memory's mind-lit monochrome?
Winged lovely moments, can I call you home?

This texture is to-day's. Near as my mind
Each instant is; yet each reveals to me
November night-falls known a lifetime long:
And I've no need to travel far to find
This bird who from the leafless walnut tree
Sings like the world's farewell to sight and song.

WEALTH OF AWARENESS

Stars burning bright in summer night; and I
Standing alone with lifetime on this lawn;
Smelling the dew that soaks the sunburnt grass,
Alone with moth-winged gloom and folded flowers
And secret stirrings, hours away from dawn.

One with these garden silences that pass,
I know that life is in my saturate sense
Of growth and memories of what lifetime meant.
I am yet young with my unheard unspent
Awareness of slow-stored intransience:
And still, where trees like sentinels look for day,
I feel what all have felt and know what none can say.

ACCEPTANCE

Can happiness be mine when the restless body tires,
And, wearied of the wine of dangerous desires,
I turn toward heights that shine with unbefriending fires?

I have looked and understood how happiness recedes;
Not like the shore we leave at sunset; not by deeds
Of anger or indifference darkened into death,
But taken away by time,—O given back like breath.

HEART AND SOUL

Growing older, the heart's not colder:
Losing youngness, the eye sees clearer.
  (Inward eye, while our sight grows blurred.)
Living longer, the soul grows stronger.
Looked on, the darkening weald grows dearer.
  (Weald of youth, a remembered word.)

Soul undaunted and heart death-haunted
Dwell together, estranged yet one.
  (Starlight lonely and firelit room.)
Heart, be brave as you go to your grave;
Soul, be girt for the race unrun.
  (Holpen both by ghosts from the gloom.)

A PICTURE OF THE MUSES

In an empty room upstairs,
While the sunshine dozes lonely
And on summer evening airs
Time is heard in rumours only,
Still unframed, my mother's 'Muses'
In their world of dawn and roses
Reinvoke an old idyllic
Rapture that my life now loses.

Long ago the flush of day-break
Bloomed beyond those calm shapes pacing.
Now, in empty room and evening,
I, that grievening vision facing,
Stand in memory's moment halted,
By my dreams no more exalted.

TRAGITONES

I have not sought these quietened cadences,
These tragitones, these stilled interior themes,
These vistas where imagined presences
Lead me away from life,—loved ghosts or dreams?

Look where the light of June is in the leaves,
And how the world with laughter hurries on.
The grass is golden; yet my faith perceives
No foot-print where felicity has gone.

MIDSUMMER EVE

Time, you timeless old mower of all that we men love most,
Are you indeed the Unknower, or a wisely garnering ghost?

On Midsummer Eve you are symbol of centuries carried like
    hay:
And all the year round you are nimble, fetching our spirits
    away
To the unknown land of death where you are a locked-out
    stranger. . . .
O Time, you bringer of breath, you ever-unchanging
    changer!

OLD WORLD TO NEW

Two thousand years ahead, maybe,
Some man looks back toward myriad Me,
And thinks, 'I'd give a lot to know
What life was like—that time ago!'

Beyond our monuments destroyed,
Beyond Utopia gained and lost,
And cheerful centuries well employed
In paying what men's folly cost,—
O face no more humane than this,
O heart no less deceived than mine,
O spirit brinked by death's abyss,
O eyes which earth and cloud confine,—
From your world order gazing back,
Learn, and forgive me what I lack.

A PRAYER FROM 1936

We are souls in hell; who hear no gradual music
Advancing on the air, on wave-lengths walking.
We are lost in life; who listen for hope and hear but
The tyrant and the politician talking.

Out of the nothingness of night they tell
Our need of guns, our servitude to strife.
O heaven of music, absolve us from this hell
Unto unmechanized mastery over life.

EARTH AND HEAVEN

What harmonies of earth are heard in heaven? . . .
If heaven there be, it is not strange nor far;
Much nearer is it than the morning star,
And human as our hearts which die forgiven.

O if there be that other world, that grace
Of souls redeemed, we breathe it like the air;
And angels are about us everywhere
In love's good deeds, in life's transfigured face.

GLORIA MUNDI

Who needs words in autumn woods
When colour concludes decay?
There old stories are told in glories
For winds to scatter away.

Wisdom narrows where downland barrows
Image the world's endeavour.
There time's tales are as light that fails
On faces fading forever.

MEETING AND PARTING

My self reborn, I look into your eyes;
While you, unknowing, look your first time on me.
Thus will *you* stand when life within me dies,
And you, full knowing, my parting presence see.

Alone I stand before my new-born son;
Alone he lies before me, doomed to live.
Beloved, when I am dying and all is done,
Look on my face and say that you forgive.

TO MY SON

Go, and be gay;
You are born into the dazzling light of day.
Go, and be wise;
You are born upon an earth which needs new eyes.
Go, and be strong;
You are born into a world where love rights wrong.
Go, and be brave;
Possess your soul; that you alone can save.

A BLESSING

Your little flame of life we guard
For the long night that must be hard:
Your eyes we teach to know the day
That shall make wonderful your way.
Bright be your flame, my soul, my son,
Whose pilgrimage I see begun:
And when these guiding hands are gone,
In love of all things good go on.

THE CHILD AT THE WINDOW

Remember this, when childhood's far away;
The sunlight of a showery first spring day;
You from your house-top window laughing down,
And I, returned with whip-cracks from a ride,
On the great lawn below you, playing the clown.
Time blots our gladness out. Let this with love abide. . . .

The brave March day; and you, not four years old,
Up in your nursery world—all heaven for me.
Remember this—the happiness I hold—
In far off springs I shall not live to see;
The world one map of wastening war unrolled,
And you, unconscious of it, setting my spirit free.

For you must learn, beyond bewildering years,
How little things beloved and held are best.
The windows of the world are blurred with tears,
And troubles come like cloud-banks from the west.
Remember this, some afternoon in spring,
When your own child looks down and makes your sad heart
    sing.

PROGRESSIONS

A lovely child alone, singing to himself serenely,—
Playing with pebbles in an unfrequented garden
Through drowse of summer afternoon where time drifts
  greenly.

A youth, impassioned by he knows not what, exploring
Delusive labyrinths in errors age will pardon,—
A youth, all ignorance, all grace, his dreams adoring.

A man, confounded by the facts of life that bind him
Prometheus-like to rocks where vulture doubts assail
  him,—
A man, with blank discarded youthfulness behind him.

A mind, matured in wearying bones, returning slowly
Toward years revisioned richly while fruitions fail him,—
A mind, renouncing hopes and finding lost loves holy.

SILLY SOOTH

Do not deny your dreams
That are the absurd release
From worldly wisdom themes
To paradoxic peace.

When sleep invites your mind
To push the unhaspèd door,
Be glad to leave behind
The unrest of Evermore.

There in that reasonless clime
You are yourself; and thither
You float, set free from Time
And all its whence and whither.

Farewell to hands and feet;
Good-bye to mouth and eyes.
Dreamer, go forth to greet
What world within you lies.

OLD MUSIC

Like the notes of an old violin,
Thoughts talk to me within
My mind, that shuttered room.
Like luminous portraits, hung
On walls where I once was young,
Dead friends pervade the gloom.

Decades of mellowing went
To make this calmed content,
This mental vintagement
Of youth's harsh tasting wine. . . .
Old violin, play on
Till heart-held thought be gone:
Old friends whose charity shone
For me, be memory-mine.

DOGGEREL ABOUT OLD DAYS

Young people now—they don't know what the past was like.
Then one could find the main roads museful on one's bike.
Give *me* a moment and I'm back in Kent; I know
How safe and sound life struck me thirty years ago.

Passenger trains puffed on through landscapes then like Time;
And this year with its next year found an easy rhyme.
Uninterrupted cricket seasons were to come.
Beanfields were good to smell and bees would always hum
In trees that knew no threat of overhead invasion.
One liked the foreground future, needing no persuasion.

Kent was all sleepy villages through which I went
Carrying my cricket-bag. In wintertime, content
To follow hounds across wet fields, I jogged home tired.
In 1909 the future was a thing desired.

I travelled on; the train was Time; Kent was the scene;
And where I was I felt that, as I'd always been,
I should continue unperturbed in storm and shine.
Will someone tell me where I am—in '39?

THE ENGLISH SPIRIT

Apollyon having decided to employ
His anger of blind armaments for this—
That every valued virtue and guarded joy
Might grieve bewildered by a bombed abyss—
    The ghosts of those who have wrought our English Past
    Stand near us now in unimpassioned ranks
    Till we have braved and broken and overcast
    The cultural crusade of Teuton tanks.

May 19, 1940.

SILENT SERVICE

Now, multifold, let Britain's patient power
Be proven within us for the world to see.
None are exempt from service in this hour;
And vanquished in ourselves we dare not be.
    Now, for a sunlit future, we can show
    The clenched resolved endurance that defies
    Daemons in dark,—and toward that future go
With earth's defended freedom in our eyes.
In every separate soul let courage shine—
A kneeling angel holding faith's front-line.

May 23, 1940.

EYES

Narcissus youth has looked at life and seen
In the strange mirror only his own stare,—
His own unanswering gaze whose circled green
Contains two tiny pictures of the scene
Where youth sits dumb, only of himself aware.

Prophetic age will bid the glass good-bye
And read his microscopic tales of being
In every face but that which answers 'I',
Earning achievement from the art of seeing.
In every face he fathoms, age will throne
The intensely sphered reflection of his own
Life-labour toward unsealed intelligence.
For life sits faithful in old eyes, alone
With mortal frailty and magnificence.